SEO for Musicians

Learn How to Promote Your Music in Search Engines to Get More Streams, Downloads, Fans, and Sales

By

Marcelo Honores

Who I am

I am an economist with 15 years in Information Technology experience plus 10 years in Internet Marketing practice. Musician by accident, I found that most musicians do not optimize their content for search engines. In addition, I realized that there are no tutorials or guides to adapt common SEO techniques to the music market needs. Therefore, I hope to fill the gap with this book and help you musicians to spread your music worldwide.

Tabla de contenido

Introduction

"The size of the independent music market is around US$ 1.4 billion per year and growing."

- Do you know that 20% of Spotify's music inventory has never been listened? (1). Indeed, around 4 million songs haven't ever received any sole stream. This means you, as an independent musician, have one chance in five to waste your work each time you publish a single or album.
- This absence of listeners is because musicians often neglect to apply Search Engine Optimization (SEO) techniques to their published work. For now SEO means the act to register music links into Search Engines' databases. As a result, fans won't be able to find your singles or albums in these websites. Certainly, SEO is an excellent promotion tool, especially for those artists with low or no marketing budget.
- In this introduction I will develop the main arguments why independent musicians should apply SEO after they publish music::
- The size of digital-music market and the share of independent musicians in the total income.

- The meaning of SEO.
- The power of SEO to promote music.
- The introduction to the SEO Framework for Musicians.
- Why this book is important for musicians and what to expect after reading the book.

The Size of the Digital-Music Market and the Share of Independent Music

The size of the global music market was US$ 16.1 billion in 2016, according to MIDIA (2). The digital-music market share was US$ 5.4 billion, according to the same source.

Big labels such as Sony, Warner, and Universal control around 70% of the digital-music market (3). The share of independent musicians was 31.3% or almost one third. Similar proportions for those musicians are in the streaming and download markets: 28.3% and 27.3% respectively. The source considers as independent musicians to those not represented by big labels. Therefore, the size of the "indie" musician market was around US$ 1.4 billion and growing.

The meaning of SEO

SEO stands for Search Engine Optimization. SEO is the art and science of notifying Search Engines such as Google, Bing or Yahoo about the existence of websites or particular web pages (or links). The purpose of this notification process is to have your links added to search engines' databases. The reason is simple; if an owner does not register his link in search engines, then people who are looking for information (through search engines) contained in that link won't find it.

In our case, the important links are those that contain our music in different online radios and stores such as Spotify, Apple Music or Deezer. Given that thousands of people use search engines every day to look for our music, informing Search Engines about the existence of our music locations is the first step to get more streams, downloads, fans, and sales.

Remember each artist, song, album or track, usually represents one link.

The power of SEO to promote music

SEO is a powerful marketing tool because there are hundreds of thousands people looking for your music through Search Engines, and right now you are not showing them your work.

For example, let's suppose you composed a love song and published it into online radios and stores. The act of publishing your single is a good starting point but is not enough. Around 550,000 people per month are actively searching love songs (see Table 1). The same occurs for romantic songs, they are 165,000 potential listeners seeking this genre.

Imagine if you could get only 1% of these fans listen to your single, this means near 5,000 listeners for love songs. For romantic songs, they might be 1,650 players. I am not including possible downloads. Note that each person is able to play your music several times per month which can give you tens of thousands streams.

Therefore, if you didn't notify Search Engines about your music, you are losing thousands of streams, downloads, fans and money. However, don't get you wrong, SEO has become rocket science. In fact, SEO implies hard work and is time consuming.

To conclude, don't worry; I am here to help you. I will teach you free and easy techniques to automate your SEO effort. This is the purpose of this book.

Table 1: Love Related Music Search Example (monthly search - worldwide)	
Keyword	Search Volume
love song	550,000
romantic song	165,000
Source: Google Keyword Planner (http://www.adwords.com)	

The SEO Framework for Musicians

The SEO Framework for Musicians (Figure 1) is the set of steps to follow to place artists' music links into Search Engines' databases and get they ranked. In this way, people will be able to find the artists' work. The reader must understand that this process is not easy, and it takes time to see the results. However, in the mid and long terms, this effort is a secure bet. In addition, I will provide training about how to automate the entire process saving the reader many hours of work. After applying these techniques, you will see an increment of visitors to your links coming from different parts of the world.

Figure 1: SEO Framework for Musicians

Summary

The purpose of the book "SEO for Musicians" is so help independent musicians without technical skills to apply SEO techniques to promote their music to a worldwide audience. Even though these practices have become difficult and expensive, in this work to perform, I chose the easiest and most automatic methods I could find. In addition, they are free to use.

I dedicate this book to those musicians not represented by big labels and that have low or no marketing budget. Furthermore, this writing may be useful for amateur musicians thinking about selling their creations in Internet. In fact, this volume is to support artists to spread their art around the world and get more streams, downloads, fans, and sales.

Stop giving your compositions for free and take a share from this US$ 1.4 billion and growing digital-music market.

References for the Introduction

(1) Rego, D. P. (2013, October 08). We've turned 5 – here's our story so far! Retrieved April 22, 2017, from https://news.spotify.com/us/2013/10/07/the-spotify-story-so-far/

(2) Global Recorded Music Revenues Grew By $1.1 Billion In 2016. (2017, March 01). Retrieved April 24, 2017, from https://www.midiaresearch.com/blog/global-recorded-music-revenues-grew-by-1-1-billion-in-2016/

(3) Global Recorded Market Music Market Shares 2016. (2017, February 27). Retrieved April 25, 2017, from https://www.midiaresearch.com/blog/global-recorded-market-music-market-shares-2016/

Part 1: Link Collection

"Each link with your music is a potential source of income."

Link collection is the first of the three processes that form the SEO framework for musicians (Figure 2). This process comprises the gathering of the links containing your creations from Internet radios and stores such as Spotify, Deezer or iTunes. Indeed, you should always remember this mantra: **Each link with your music is a potential source of income**. Therefore, in the next paragraphs, I will expose the three main steps of the link collection process:

- First, I will introduce the online radio and store landscape.
- Then, I will give some tactics to prioritize and select radios and stores to promote.
- Finally, I will explain how to gather your music links.

Figure 2: SEO Framework for Musicians – Link
Collection

Prerequisites for This Chapter

Before reading this chapter you should verify that your music complains the following two conditions:

Be sure that your music is already available in online radios and stores.

If you didn't place your compositions in online radios and stores yet, you should deliver them through a music distribution service. Here you have a sample list of distributors. However, before submit your work, check their business model. Each applies different commission's structure to royalties. Choose the one most convenient for you.

- CD Baby.
- TuneCore.
- Ditto Music.
- Loudr.
- Record Union.
- MondoTunes.
- Symphonic.

Be sure that your music has YouTube's Content Id

Content Id (1) is an identification that YouTube assigns to each piece of music uploaded with a video. Getting this identification is very important because YouTube is one of the biggest sources of income for musicians. Usually, music distributors hide or sell separately the YouTube distribution service. Therefore, double check this feature.

An easy way to verify is to upload a simple video with your music to YouTube. If the music has Content Id, this video service will give you a warning showing the name of the artist and the title of the song. Hopefully, this will be your song, if it is not, you will be in trouble. If you have doubts, ask your distributor support.

The Online Radio and Store Landscape

When you publish your creation through a distribution service, This will deliver it to online radios and stores, most of them included in Table 2. After that, your work is to collect the links from each radio and store to notify Search Engines about the existence of the web pages. As a result, music fans will be able to find your web assets. Later, in the next chapter, I will explain the notification process. For now, let's focus on the collection one.

As you can see in Table 2, the list of Internet radios and stores is huge. Therefore, I understand that collecting all links at once may be a heavy task. However, don't panic yet, I am here to help you. The key is to apply the SEO framework for musicians, starting from the most important services to the less important ones, one by one. To address this problem, I will show several criteria to prioritize and select the most popular radios and stores to collect links first.

Table 2: Online Radios and Stores

Radio	Stream	Download
1 24-7	Yes	Yes
2 7digital	Yes	Yes
3 8tracks	Yes	No
4 Akazoo	Yes	Yes
5 Amazon MP3 (1)	Yes	Yes
6 Apple iTunes (1)	Yes	Yes
7 AWA	Yes	No
8 Deezer	Yes	Yes
9 eMusic	No	Yes
10 Google Music Store	Yes	Yes
11 Groove	Yes	Yes
12 iHeartRadio	Yes	Yes
13 Inprodicon	No	No
14 kkbox	Yes	No
15 Kuack	Yes	No
16 Line Music	Yes	No
17 Pandora	Yes	No
18 Rhapsody	Yes	Yes
19 Saavn	Yes	No
20 Slacker Radio	Yes	No
21 Spotify	Yes	No
22 Tidal	Yes	Yes
23 Tradebit	No	Yes
24 Yandex	Yes	No
25 YouTube Music	Yes	No

(1) Download and streaming services in different stores

Source: Author's data

Criteria to Prioritize and Select Online Radios and Stores to Collect Links

I recognize that collecting all the links from all online radios and stores at once is a huge task. Therefore, we should prioritize and select which web properties to work first.

In that sense, I found four criteria to select links for promotion: the type of service, the number of subscribers, and by pay-per-stream:

• Selecting online radios and stores according to the type of website:

There are five types of services on the Internet:

- Music streaming
- Music downloads,
- Mixed streaming and downloads
- Music databases, and
- Royalty management services.

Then, in Table 2 I discarded already, music databases and royalty management services such as Medianet and Sound Exchange because they don't sell music directly.

• Selecting online radios and stores according to the number of paid subscribers:

From the Figure 3, you can appreciate the most popular radios ranked by the number of paid subscribers.

19

Figure 3: paid subscriptions by online radio or store (2)

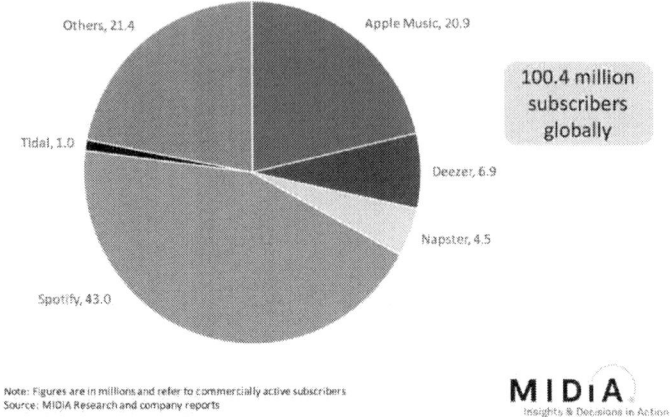

Spotify Continues To Dominate Streaming Subscriptions With 43% Market Share

Global Streaming Music Subscribers, December 2016

Others, 21.4

Apple Music, 20.9

100.4 million subscribers globally

Tidal, 1.0

Deezer, 6.9

Napster, 4.5

Spotify, 43.0

Note: Figures are in millions and refer to commercially active subscribers
Source: MIDiA Research and company reports

MIDiA
Insights & Decisions in Action

Note: The total paid subscribers were around 100 million users in 2016

From the Figure 3 we can build a draft list:

- Spotify (43%)
- Apple Music (20.9%)
- Deezer (6.9%)

Remember that you are free to add or remove services according to your own criteria.

• Selecting online radios and stores according to the number of free subscribers:

Even it is not a specific audio streaming service, YouTube accounts for the 46% of all music streaming listening time worldwide excluding China (2).

20

Therefore, this video service should be the first web asset to work first with, in despite the fact that it pays far less that other music streaming ones. However, what you don't get in fares you get in volume. Indeed, YouTube is my first source of income and it should be yours.

Unfortunately, there are not clear statistics about paid and free subscribers, but Figure 4 gives us a clear path. From this graphic, I can discard the following radios: Pandora, because is a music recommendation engine; SoundCloud, because there is no way to earn money from it. I also get rid of IHeartRadio; NPR One, and Tune In because they broadcast AM/FM radios.

This removal is in despite of their popularity and the reason is the difficulty to get the links from these services:

Figure 4: Audio streaming service survey 2017 (3)

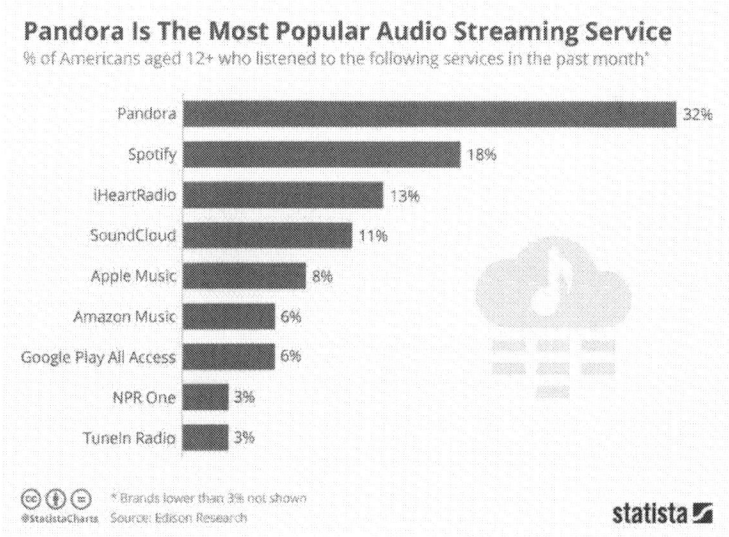

Pandora Is The Most Popular Audio Streaming Service
% of Americans aged 12+ who listened to the following services in the past month*

Service	%
Pandora	32%
Spotify	18%
iHeartRadio	13%
SoundCloud	11%
Apple Music	8%
Amazon Music	6%
Google Play All Access	6%
NPR One	3%
TuneIn Radio	3%

* Brands lower than 3% not shown
@StatistaCharts Source: Edison Research

statista

• Selecting online radios by pay-per-stream royalty:

In online music business, there are two ways to earn money: by purchasing downloads and streams.

Considering downloads; the prices are similar in online stores. On average, the price per album is around is US$ 9 and per single US$ 0.9. Therefore, your royalties will be around US$ 7 and US$ 0.7 respectively after commissions. This is an approximation with little variations according to the store and the commission rate of your music distributor.

In that sense, I recommend you to work first with the main download stores such as Amazon and Google Play and not losing time on small ones because downloading services will decline as streaming become principal. However, you can start to apply SEO later to less important stores after you finish with the big ones. Remember, each link with your music is a potential source of income.

Regarding streams, royalties vary from radio to radio. In Table 3, you can see average payments by online radios. Royalty varies for several reasons. To illustrate, in some countries the radios pay better than others. The best royalties come from European countries, following by those from USA, the Americas, and Asia, with some exceptions such as Singapore, Taiwan, and Japan. Royalties vary also because some radios have free and paid plans for subscribers such as Spotify and Deezer. Therefore, these radios have different payments per-stream.

Table 3: Pay Per Stream And Store (2016)

	Radio	Pay per stream (US$)
1	**Stream average**	0.0049
2	Groove	0.0350
3	iTunes Apple Music - Norway	0.0228
4	iTunes Apple Music - Denmark	0.0183
5	iTunes Apple Music - Switzerland	0.0163
6	iTunes Apple Music - United Kingdom	0.0142
7	iTunes Apple Music Australia	0.0117
8	Tidal	0.0106
9	iTunes Apple Music - New Zealand	0.0103
10	iTunes Apple Music - Japan	0.0103
11	Rhapsody	0.0098
12	iTunes Apple Music - Hong Kong	0.0094
13	iTunes Apple Music - Singapore	0.0090
14	iTunes Apple Music - US	0.0079
15	JB Hi-Fi	0.0074
16	iTunes Apple Music - Europe	0.0073
17	Slacker Radio	0.0071
18	Google Music Store	0.0065
19	iTunes Apple Music - Rest of World	0.0059
20	iTunes Apple Music - Canada	0.0056
21	iTunes Apple Music - South Africa	0.0051
22	iTunes Apple Music - Indonesia	0.0050
23	Simfy	0.0043
24	Deezer	0.0042
25	Spotify	0.0039
26	YouTube Music	0.0037
27	iTunes Apple Music - Sweden	0.0022
28	iTunes Apple Music - Russia	0.0021
29	Yandex	0.0010
30	8tracks	0.0002

Source: Author's data

Consequently, we are seeing a consolidation of the online radio market and the emergence of streaming as the main source of fans and income. As a result, you should put your effort in promoting your radio links.

Introduction Web Scraping

Web Scraping means the act to collect links from a website manually or using a piece of software. In this case, you will need the following data from your music links:

- The name of the song.
- The URL of the song.
- The URL of the image or artwork, and
- The artist or group name.

Extracting manually links for online radios and stores

This is the easiest way. In almost all radio apps, you can get your link from the share button or more easily from the address bar, if you are in a web interface. YouTube is a particular case that I will explain later.

Automating link extraction for online radios and stores

If you have few creations in online stores you can extract links manually. However, if you have tens of music pieces online, you will need tools that help you with this task. Here a list of browser extensions that you can use for free to scrape you web links:

Name	Pricing		Handle Large Volumes?
Data Scraper	Free	Chrome Extension	No
Web Scraper	Free	Chrome Extension	Yes
Scraper	Free	Chrome Extension	No
Grepsr r	Free	Chrome Extension	No

OutwitHub	Free	Firefox Extension/	No
		Desktop Application	
FMiner	Free	Desktop Application	No

To find them visit the Chrome Store (https://chrome.google.com), search the extension and install it. Then read the documentation, watch the videos and start to scrap your music properties.

If you want to experiment with other extensions, search for "visual web scraper" or "visual web scrapping."

Other similar tool:
http://webscraper.io

In case you think it is too difficult the use of these tools or if you have hundreds of songs, you can one of the outsourcing services described in the **resources section** of the book.

I have crawlers for:
- Spotify
- iTunes
- Deezer
- Amazon

Extracting links from YouTube

YouTube is a particular case. Even though you can apply the methods explained to extract links. The problem with YouTube is that it does not create videos by default when you deliver your music via music distributors. You must create a video for each piece of music you compose.

But don't worry; to get advantage of YouTube you don't need to create an expensive video clip, you can make a simple one with just an image and your music on it. Indeed, you find see thousands of videos with thousands of streams in that format. The key is the promotion.

As an alternative, you can postpone the work with YouTube and start with the other assets.

Summary for Part 1: Link Collection

Finally, here is my recommended list to start to apply SEO:

- Youtube
- Spotify
- Apple Music
- Deezer
- Amazon
- Google Play

Remember again that you are free to add or remove radios and stores to this list, or change the order.

Even though link collection is a heavy task, the advice here is to prioritize the extracting work with the most important radios and stores first. Even better, you might work radio by radio and link by link to avoid overwhelming yourself.

Later, you can continue promoting the rest of radios and stores with the same methodology we will apply to this list. Moreover, you can promote the main services first, and then, once you receive income, you can outsource the rest of services to freelancers.

In the next chapter, I will show examples with the above websites. However, the method is the same if you want to work with the rest of radios and stores.

References of Part 1: Link Collection

(1) YouTube Monetization. (n.d.). Retrieved September 07, 2017, from http://rumblefish.com/youtube-monetization/

(2) Music Business Worldwide. (2018, April 30). More music is played on YouTube than on Spotify, Apple Music and every other audio streaming platform combined. Retrieved from https://www.musicbusinessworldwide.com/more-music-is-played-on-youtube-than-on-spotify-apple-music-and-every-audio-streaming-platform-combined/

(3) McCarthy, N. (2017, March 14). Infographic: Pandora Is The Most Popular Audio Streaming Service. Retrieved April 24, 2017, from https://www.statista.com/chart/8503/pandora-is-the-most-popular-audio-streaming-service/

Part 2: Link Indexing

"In conclusion, the objective of link indexing is to place your paying and supporting links before useless and competitor's ones in Search Engine results"

Link indexing is the act of notifying Search Engines such as Google, Bing, or Yahoo about the appearance a new web page. The purpose is to get your links included into their databases. In this way, your web properties will appear in searchers' results when someone is looking for similar music. Usually, Search Engines index new pages from a website automatically, but not always include all the ones, just a small sample, especially when the pages look alike. In our case, full indexing of our links requires human intervention.

In Part I, I suggested a list of the six main radios and online stores to start with. Then, you can apply what you learnt here to the rest of smaller radios and stores included in Table 2. Given that indexing is different for each radio and store, in the next paragraphs, I will explain each case in depth. Indeed, the primary list contains the following sites:

1. YouTube
2. Spotify
3. Apple Music
4. Deezer

5. Amazon
6. Google Play

Before we start the indexing process, let's make some important definitions. From the SEO point of view, there are three types of links:

- **Money links**: Links containing your music in legitimate radios and stores, the ones that will pay you royalties, for example, those appearing in Table 2.
- **Support links**: Links pointing out our money links that are the result from the link ranking process I will explan later.
- **Useless links**: Web links with competitive music, spam, piracy and not related with our web properties.

Checking If Your Artist, Single or Album Link Is Indexed

Let's suppose you have the following song link:

- https://open.spotify.com/album/5RdfxhR8xWsfa0cY2YLkH4

To check if you link is indexed by google use this command:

- info:https://open.spotify.com/album/5RdfxhR8xWsfa0cY2YLkH4

There is a practical way to know if a Search Engine such as Google, Bing or Yahoo and type has indexed your content. Just type in your preferred search engine:

- *"Your title song" Your Artist or Group Name*

For example, I have two singles; one published three years ago and another published one month ago. Therefore, the search for the old one would be:

- *"Lucid Dreaming" meditaudios*

This search gives me 2,010 results.

The search for the new one

- *"Baroque Flow" meditaudios*

This search gives me 17 results. However, you are looking not only for the quantity of links but also for their quality. Thus, in the old single, I got the following results in the first page of Google:

1. https://www.cdbaby.com/cd/meditaudios12
2. https://www.amazon.com/Lucid-Dreaming...
3. https://open.spotify.com/track/4GPvd2TKXE05cC DdKZdCPP
4. https://itunes.apple.com/us/album/lucid-dreaming...
5. https://SoundCloud.com/meditaudios/meditaudi os-theta4-bb-5-noise
6. https://www.iheart.com/artist/meditaudios-30056879/albums/lucid...
7. http://ar.napster.com/artist/meditaudios/album/l ucid...
8. https://www.YouTube.com/watch?v=u7S2MqQJjl 8
9. http://mp3host.top/mp3?ids=187048430
10. https://www.amazon.co.jp/dp/B00H8LYXZW/ref= dm_ws_tlw_trk1

On the other hand, in the new single I got the

following results:

1. https://www.amazon.com/Baroque-Flow...
2. https://za.pinterest.com/pin/7053763603576140
   77
3. http://www.YouTube.com/watch?v=rNCVabfriv4
4. http://www.YouTube.com/watch?v=fG51HHF2a5I
5. http://www.YouTube.com/watch?v=K7Pe8W3mA
   SE
6. https://themusic.today/release/meditaudios-
   baroque-flow...
7. http://www.cdbaby.com/m/artist/Meditaudios1
8. https://itunes.apple.com/us/artist/meditaudios/i
   d778919518
9. https://SoundCloud.com/mentallion
10. http://animeniach.com/mp3/trance-music-
   example.html

In the old single example, I show the results classified according to the three types of links defined before:

Money sites:

- https://www.cdbaby.com/cd/meditaudios12
- https://www.amazon.com/Lucid-Dreaming...
- https://open.spotify.com/track/4GPvd2TKXE05cC
  DdKZdCPP
- https://itunes.apple.com/us/album/lucid-
  dreaming...
- https://www.iheart.com/artist/meditaudios-
  30056879/albums/lucid...
- http://ar.napster.com/artist/meditaudios/album/l
  ucid...
- https://www.amazon.co.jp/dp/B00H8LYXZW/ref=
  dm_ws_tlw_trk1

Support sites:

- https://SoundCloud.com/meditaudios/meditaudios-theta4-bb-5-noise
- https://www.YouTube.com/watch?v=u7S2MqQJjI8

Useless site (not related or spam):

- http://mp3host.top/mp3?ids=187048430

In the second case, here are the results:

Money sites:

- https://www.amazon.com/Baroque-Flow...
- http://www.cdbaby.com/m/artist/Meditaudios1
- https://itunes.apple.com/us/artist/meditaudios/id778919518

Support sites:

- https://za.pinterest.com/pin/705376360357614077
- https://themusic.today/release/meditaudios-baroque-flow...
- https://SoundCloud.com/mentallion
- http://animeniach.com/mp3/trance-music-example.html

Useless site (not related or spam)

- http://www.YouTube.com/watch?v=K7Pe8W3mASE
- http://www.YouTube.com/watch?v=fG51HHF2a5I
- http://www.YouTube.com/watch?v=rNCVabfriv4

In conclusion, the objective of link indexing is to place your paying and supporting links before useless and competitor's ones in Search Engine results

How Monitor the Link Indexing Process

Monitoring the link indexing process is an important step to check the progress of your work when you apply the SEO Framework for Musicians. Happily, there is an easy way to monitor in real time the indexing process. Just go to https://www.google.com/alerts and create an alert with the title of your single or album plus the artist name and target your email to receive the news.

Creating the alert is similar to checking the existence of that link in search engines. Just use this format:

- *"Your title song" Your Artist or Group Name*

For example:

- *"Baroque Flow" meditaudios*

Each time any of your links is indexed you will receive an email alert with information about that event.

How to Index Links

Firs, I want to introduce the term "ping." Ping is a term borrowed from the computer networking field and means the act to test if a server is running. In SEO, ping means the act of notifying a Search Engine the existence of a particular link for its posterior indexing.

In the following paragraphs, I will present three ways to index web links: The easy way that involves the use of a specialized website. The medium-difficult way, in case the first website disappears. Finally, a manual one in case you need finer graining indexing.

The easy way to index links

After you collect your links (I will explain this process step by step later) you can submit your link to this website;

- http://www.linkcentaur.com

This service is free up to 50 links per day, enough for most needs. Just signup, create a project, copy and paste your links, and press the submit button. Then wait some days and your links will start to appear. You can find other paid link indexing services in search engines just look for the term "link indexing service."

Medium difficult indexing

Given that websites often appear and disappear frequently, I will give you some alternatives in case LinkCentaur.com ceases to exist.

Look for the term "mass ping" without quotes in a Search Engine, you will find many alternatives such as:

- http://www.pingbomb.com
- http://ninjaseotools.com/mass-ping.php
- http://pingfarm.com
- http://www.massping.org
- http://www.mass-ping.com

Be sure to choose the one that supports the pinging of many links at the same time. Just choose one of the above links, paste your kinks and press the submit button. There should not be a number of link limitations per day, but I recommend indexing your links in portions.

More difficult indexing

You can submit your link directly to each Search Engine, but this process is difficult because you have to go to each Search Engine and submit one link at the time. If you have tens of links, this process is painful. Here some Search Engine submission links:

1. Google:

https://www.google.com/webmasters/tools/submit -url

2. Bing:

https://www.bing.com/toolbox/submit-site-url

3. Yahoo

https://search.yahoo.com/info/submit.html

4. Yandex (Russian Search Engine)

https://webmaster.yandex.com/site/indexing/reind ex/

5. Baidu (Chinese Search Engine)

http://zhanzhang.baidu.com

Indexing Spotify Links

There are two ways of collecting your links from Spotify: The first is login to Spotify, find your music artist, single, album or track, click the 3 points button and select the option to copy the link. Alternative, you can copy the browser's address. In Spotify, there are four types of links.

Example link for an artist;

- https://open.spotify.com/**artist**/68jjoghycp9jnGP W2eFbon

Example link for an album;

- https://open.spotify.com/**album**/56uMxYKZYpIRw keBoXJ9I8

Example link for a single;

- https://open.spotify.com/**album**/5RdfxhR8xWsfa0 cY2YLkH4

Example link for a track;

- https://open.spotify.com/**track**/350MZs4tZZc08u dtK8Lhr1

Example for an entire album (12 songs):

1. https://open.spotify.com/**album**/7zici5GP9pYdLkP VL1gSgq
2. https://open.spotify.com/**track**/3sCAOCbR16HSO 8aaRF0yte
3. https://open.spotify.com/**track**/5vrYcOajiL6O84H z5bUYrB
4. https://open.spotify.com/**track**/5pzZCwpUCo3mU

AD67ZG885

5. https://open.spotify.com/**track**/41aWSoc3CiOLSL
p1PCrOtV
6. https://open.spotify.com/**track**/1pBloATzGSgDFFF
R33c8d8
7. https://open.spotify.com/**track**/6kTob9CWOCYM
Nbm8GjRG1N
8. https://open.spotify.com/**track**/3tjKuQTlgOYwK5s
dOOpkqv
9. https://open.spotify.com/**track**/4hl7HeullwMHDV
0aWUunMO
10. https://open.spotify.com/**track**/3YqM71a7ylWf6O
0OS5WKsw
11. https://open.spotify.com/**track**/5QdZYM5Kwh8Cd
brhCbgcOu
12. https://open.spotify.com/**track**/0iiHrxQHgAmE38
B4CfpvB6
13. https://open.spotify.com/**track**/0hXGq4HR93lgYU
CiKwD3Tm

Note: choose the prefix "open" over "play", because
"open" works with apps and websites, while "play"
works only with websites.

This method works fine for a small amount of singles
and albums.

The second method is advisable only if you have tens
or more singles and albums. As a consequence, you
will have tens of links. Thus, you may want to get all
of them at once. In that sense, I recommend hiring a
paid service. In the resource's section of this book,
there is a list of recommended services to download
all your links from Spotify and some other online
radios and stores.

Once you got the links, you can copy them and paste
in one of the indexing services described before.

To conclude, do not forget to index your artist link. For a single, you just need to gather one link only. If you have an album with 10 tracks, you have to gather the link of your album plus the 10 links of your tracks. Therefore, indexing an entire album takes 11 links.

Indexing iTunes Links

Indexing iTunes links is different than do the same with Spotify. ITunes has 155 regional stores (2). Therefore, if you want to get listeners from around the world, you should index all the 155 links plus the neutral link where your music is available.

ITunes uses the ISO 3166-1 alpha-2 codes (1) notation to differentiate its stores. Therefore, for each artist, single, album or track you may need the neutral link plus 155 variations. Here is an example, but for brevity, I show only four variations:

For an artist:

- Neutral version:

https://itunes.apple.com/**artist**/goodvibras/id6470512 82

- Albania:

https://itunes.apple.com/**al**/artist/goodvibras/id647051 282

- Canada:

https://itunes.apple.com/**ca**/artist/goodvibras/id64705 1282

- USA:

https://itunes.apple.com/**us**/artist/goodvibras/id64705
1282

- Zimbabwe:

https://itunes.apple.com/**zw**/artist/goodvibras/id64705
1282

For a single:

- Neutral version:

https://itunes.apple.com/**album**/creative-thinking-
development-10hz-isochronic-tones/id838262184

- Albania:

https://itunes.apple.com/**al**/album/creative-thinking-
development-10hz-isochronic-tones/id838262184

- Canada:

https://itunes.apple.com/**ca**/album/creative-thinking-
development-10hz-isochronic-tones/id838262184

6. USA:

https://itunes.apple.com/**us**/album/creative-thinking-
development-10hz-isochronic-tones/id838262184

7. Zimbabwe:

https://itunes.apple.com/**zw**/album/creative-thinking-
development-10hz-isochronic-tones/id838262184

To conclude, you should index always your artist link
in the neutral format plus the other 155 regional

variations. Therefore, you should index in total 156 links. For each single is the same effort. If you have an album with 10 songs, you have to collect the 156 links from your album plus the 1,560 links from your 10 tracks. In total, you have to index 1,716 links for an entire album.

Yes, this process looks like a difficult task, but it's necessary to differentiate your music from your rivals' one. This work of generating regional links can be easily done in a spreadsheet. However, if you don't have time for this, you can find services that will make this work for you in the book's resources section.

Indexing Deezer Links

Similar to iTunes, Deezer has 187 regional variations of its website (2). Deezer uses the same codification as iTunes. Therefore, to index these web properties, you have to use the neutral version of each link plus the 187 link variations to index them.

There are two ways of collecting your links here: The first is login to Deezer, find your music artist, single, album or track, click the 3 points button and select the option share the link. Alternative, you can copy the browser's address. In Deezer, there are four types of links:

Example link for an artist:

- http://www.deezer.com/**artist**/5674360

Example link for an artist in US store:

- http://www.deezer.com/**us**/artist/5674360

Example link for a single:

- http://www.deezer.com/**album**/8402432

Example link for a single in US store:

- http://www.deezer.com/**us**/album/8402432

Example link for a track;

- http://www.deezer.com/**track**/126132053

Example link for a track in US store;

- http://www.deezer.com/**us**/track/126132053

Example for an entire album in neutral version (12 songs):

1. http://www.deezer.com/album/13277189
2. http://www.deezer.com/track/126132049
3. http://www.deezer.com/track/126132051
4. http://www.deezer.com/track/126132053
5. http://www.deezer.com/track/126132055
6. http://www.deezer.com/track/126132057
7. http://www.deezer.com/track/126132059
8. http://www.deezer.com/track/126132061
9. http://www.deezer.com/track/126132063
10. http://www.deezer.com/track/126132065
11. http://www.deezer.com/track/126132067
12. http://www.deezer.com/track/126132069

http://www.deezer.com/track/126132071

To conclude, you should index always your artist link in the neutral format plus the other 187 regional variations. Therefore, you should index in total 188 links. For each single is the same effort. If you have an album with 10 songs, you have to collect the 188 links from your album plus the 1,880 links from your 10 tracks. In total, you have to index 2,068 links for an entire album.

Again, this process looks like a difficult task, but it's necessary to differentiate your music from your rivals' one. This work of generating regional links can be easily done in a spreadsheet. However, if you don't have time for this, you can find services that will make this work for you in the book's resources section.

Indexing Amazon Links

At the time of writing this book, Amazon has 12 stores (4).

1. Brazil: http://www.amazon.com.br
2. Canada: http://www.amazon.ca
3. China: http://www.amazon.cn
4. France: http://www.amazon.fr
5. Germany: http://www.amazon.de
6. India: http://www.amazon.in/
7. Italy: http://www.amazon.it
8. Japan: http://www.amazon.co.jp
9. Mexico: http://www.amazon.com.mx
10. Spain: http://www.amazon.es
11. United Kingdom: http://www.amazon.co.uk/
12. United States: http://www.amazon.com

Therefore, your work here is to find your music link in each store and indexing. Note that your music not always will be available in each store.

For example, for the group Goodvibras, I have links in the following Amazon stores;

1. https://www.amazon.com/Goodvibras/e/B00OTV
DAKS/digital/
2. https://www.amazon.co.uk/Goodvibras/e/B00OT
VDAKS/digital/
3. https://www.amazon.es/s/ref=ntt_srch_rd_B00O
TVDAKS
4. https://www.amazon.co.jp/Goodvibras/e/B00OTV
DAKS/digital/
5. https://www.amazon.de/Goodvibras/e/B00OTVD
AKS /digital /
6. https://www.amazon.fr/Goodvibras/e/B00OTVDA
KS/digital/

However, I have no data in these stores;

- https://www.amazon.com.mx
- http://www.amazon.in
- https://www.amazon.cn
- https://www.amazon.com.br
- https://www.amazon.ca

As a result, for the single: Renaissance Flow of Goodvibras, I have 6 links:

- https://www.amazon.com/dp/B06Y1K5BYV/
- https://www.amazon.co.uk/dp/B06Y29XNGN/
- https://www.amazon.es/Renaissance-Flow-Modern-Music-Example/dp/B06Y27YCVK/
- https://www.amazon.co.jp/dp/B06Y1L1ZTP/
- https://www.amazon.de/dp/B06Y27NTQ2/
- https://www.amazon.fr/dp/B06Y1ZK487/

As a summary, it is advisable to index the 6 versions of your artist link. Do the same for each single. If you have an album with 10 songs you have to gather 6 links from your album plus the 60 links from your tracks, in total 66 links.

Indexing Google Play

Indexing Google Play links is easier because this store has not neither album track links nor regional ones. You just need to collect your artist, singles, and albums links.

- For the Goodvibras artist link example, you have the following link:

https://play.google.com/store/music/artist/Goodvibras?id=A4gkiuebqyp7n2jh4bsh2u6sioe

- For the single Renaissance Flow:

https://play.google.com/store/music/album/Goodvibras_Renaissance_Flow_Modern_Renaissance_Mus?id=Babt6rke7v3kp5vnkudpc2s4mr4

- For the album Natural Anxiety Remedies:

https://play.google.com/store/music/album/Goodvibras_Natural_Anxiety_Remedies_Anxiety_Instan?id=Bidpwdigsfbczoo2e6m2c75ihtu

In summary, in the Google Play store you need to collect only one link for the artist link, one link per single, and one link per album.

Regarding YouTube Links

When you hire a music distribution service to deliver your music to online radios and stores, you should verify that this service includes YouTube in your order. This step is necessary because some content distributors sell this service separately. Another thing you need from your music distributor is to get a synchronization license for each of your songs. Ask your music distributor about these features.

An easy way to test if your music has Content Id is to upload a simple video with your music embedded in it. If your music is registered already, YouTube will send you a warning with the artist's name and the song's title; hopefully, it will be your artist name. If the warning contains a different artist name than yours, you will be in trouble; another person registered your song. In this case, you must file a claim, but the procedure escapes the scope of this book. If there is no warning, it means that your song is available for registration. In this last case, ask immediately your music distributor to register your song in YouTube. There are also online services that get the Content Id from YouTube for you.

Regarding YouTube, this service has two versions: a free service that we all know about and a paid one: YouTube Red. Therefore, the links from the latter are the ones that matter for SEO purposes. If you want to index these links you should subscribe to YouTube Red, the paid service. Then, get the links and index them. However, you should not worry too much about. YouTube belongs to Google and it regularly catalogs its own content. Nevertheless, indexing your links as described before will help other search engines to include your content giving more exposure to your work.

As I mentioned before, having the Content Id is crucial to get royalties from your music, because YouTube is the world's biggest streaming service. It has a billion views per day so be sure your music will be listened eventually.

About SoundCloud and similar websites

As a rule, I never submit my music to Sounrcloud before deliver it to online radios and stores via music distributors. The reason is that there is too much piracy on the Internet, if you deliver your song without copyright protection, any people may register for you and get your royalties. Once protected your music, you can submit it to SoundCloud because it is a great source of backings for your music as we will see in the Part 3: Link Ranking.

The same reasoning applies for similar websites such as Bandcamp, Reverbnation, Mixcloud, etc.

Summary for Part 2: Link Indexing

After reading this chapter, you know how to index your links in search engines. The more links you index, the more visits your links will start to get. Indeed, the fact to index your content will increase the visits to you web properties. However, to get even more visits, you should start to rank your web properties in search engines. That process will be explained in the next chapter.

Resources for Part 2 Link Indexing

(1) Nationsonline.org, K. K. (n.d.). List of Country Codes :: Nations Online Project. Retrieved April 29, 2017, from http://www.nationsonline.org/oneworld/country_code_list.htm

(2) ITunes Country Stores. (2017, March 27). Retrieved August 21, 2017, from https://developer.apple.com/library/content/document ation/LanguagesUtilities/Conceptual/iTunesConnect_ Guide/Chapters/AppStoreTerritories.html

(3) Deezer Available Regions. (n.d.). Retrieved August 02, 2017, from https://developers.deezer.com/guidelines/countries

(4) Amazon stores: Retrieved April 29, 2017, from http://docs.aws.amazon.com/AWSECommerceService /latest/DG/Locales.html

(5) Microsoft Groove Worldwide Sites. (n.d.). Retrieved August 02, 2017, from https://www.microsoft.com/en-us/groove/worldwide.aspx

.

Part 3: Link Ranking

Think the Internet as a democratic nation. People vote for webpages through their activity there."..."For online radios, the vote is the stream. For online stores, the vote is the purchase. For search engines, the vote is the backlink."

Link Ranking is the last process of the **SEO Framework for Musicians** (Figure 4). This process it is about scaling in search engine results.

Figure 4: SEO Framework for Musicians – Link Ranking

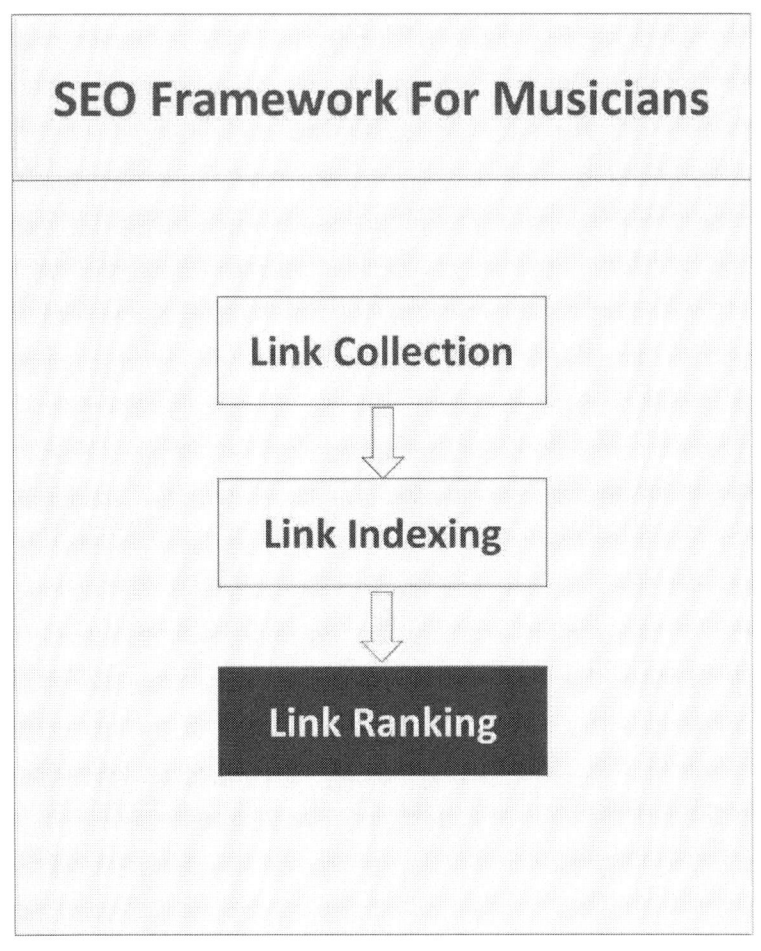

For example, when a fan queries for a piece of music in a search engine, the latter shows a list of links grouped by pages containing 10 links items per page (Figure 5). However, before showing them to the user, search engines sort the results according to certain SEO factors I will explicate later.

If you didn't index your web pages before, search

engines won't even show any of them on the result pages. If you just indexed them, search engines will show your web properties in the last pages of the search results, far from the top ones where most people arrive. Finally, once you start ranking your links you will find them in the first pages of search engines, where most potential clients land.

Therefore, the process' purpose is to move your music links from last pages, where few people reach, to the top ones, where arrive the most. If your work appears in the first result's pages, the probability that fans take an action is higher, for example, they may stream or buy your creations. This climbing through search results happens by working hard over the SEO factors I will explain in the next paragraphs.

Something similar occurs with online radios and stores. Each one includes an internal search engine. Each search engine shows outcomes sorted according to its own ranking factors. Therefore, to rank your compositions in search engines from Internet radios and stores, we need to address different ranking factors than those on pure search engines such as Google, Bing or Baidu, to scale our music to higher positions.

Figure 5: Link Ranking in Search Engines

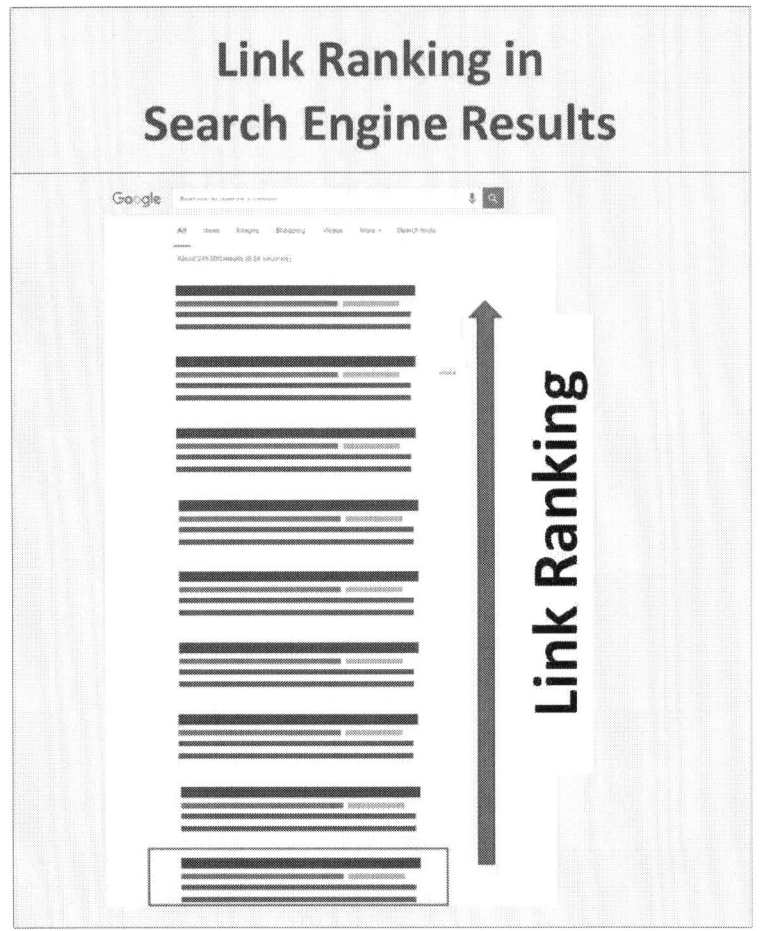

SEO factors to Rank Links: The Democratic Strategy

Think the Internet as a democratic nation. People vote for web pages through their activity there. The more activity has a web page, the more popular it is. The activity is the vote or, in this case, the SEO factor. This activity varies from website to website. For online radios, the vote is the stream. For online stores, the vote is the purchase. For search engines, the vote is the backlink. To conclude, the SEO factors to work with are: streams, purchases, and backlinks for radios, stores, and search engines respectively.

It is true that the factors to rank web pages described above, are not the only ones, but they are the main ones. Therefore, in the next lines, I will focus on these factors and propose you some tactics to rank webpages in each type of website.

Tactics to rank in Online Stores

I focus on online stores first, because the democratic strategy is the easiest to implement. In this case, the vote is the purchase and the ranking factor. Therefore, you should start to vote for your own music by purchasing it. Consider online stores as search engines. They rank products mainly by the number of purchases. The same happens with music. Consequently, the strategy is simple: just eat your own food. When you publish a single or album in stores such as Amazon, Google Play, iTunes, etc., you should be the first one to buy your music in each store. As a result, your song will rank better than the thousands of songs that have never been bought.

Indeed, 99 cents for buying a single won't hurt you. For an album, you should buy at least one track. Definitely, this purchase will help to improve your rankings in online stores.

Tactics to rank in Online Radios

The democratic strategy also works to rank your music in online radios. Here, the stream is the vote and the ranking factor. Again, you should start voting for your own work by streaming it. However, you can enrich the implementation by following these steps: first, get a second-hand computer or laptop; then, start a browser and open several tabs; finally, start to listen to your music full-time in as many radios as you can simultaneously. If you cannot afford to dedicate a computer to that task full time because you use it to work in day-hours, play your music during the night. You should do this the first weeks after you launched your single or album to give it a basic push. Don't abuse of this tactic as it will look like spam. You can empower this tactic with the use of playlists, a tactic I will explain later.

Learn How Monitor your SEO Rankings

Before I explain you how to rank in search engines, you should learn how to check the current positions of your links. To track the ranking of your links, try any of these websites:

- https://www.searchenginegenie.com/google-rank-checker.html
- https://smallseotools.com/keyword-position/

- http://cuterank.net/
- https://serps.com/tools/rank-checker/

Once there, input the link of your song as the URL and the title as the keyword. Try entering the title with quotes if it has more than one word. These websites show if your web page is into the first 100 results..

If none of your links appears, maybe your website is not indexed yet. In this case, read again the Part 2 of this book, index your link, and wait some days.

If any of your links appear, check the position, and start working in the tactics I will show below. Then, check the rankings monthly to observe the progress. I must warn you that this process is slow but rewarding in the long-term. Remember that you have to rank the links that you got from the different radios and stores.

Tactics to Rank in Search Engines

You should know you can rank your music in online radios in parallel to search engines. The tactics to scale in both sides are complementary not exclusive. On one hand, you get listeners from usual users from web broadcasters. On the other hand, you get listeners searching specifically your genre.

The traditional tasks to climb positions in Search Engines are difficult and time-consuming. That's why SEO is a billionaire industry today because it requires specialized agencies. However, I will show you some free, simple, and automate tactics ascend your web properties on autopilot.

Search engines want what I call "SEO noise." This means they like your links appear in different well-established and popular websites. That is what SEO **professionals call** "backlinks". Therefore, let's give search engines what they like.

Getting Backlinks from This Unknown Music Social Network

Last.fm is a great SEO tool for musicians. This website allows any music fan to share her streams with the world in real time. This sharing process is known as "scrobble" (1). In addition, once your music appears in this website, it allows you to document about your artists, singles, and albums (Figure 6).

Figure 6: Automating Link Ranking with Last.fm

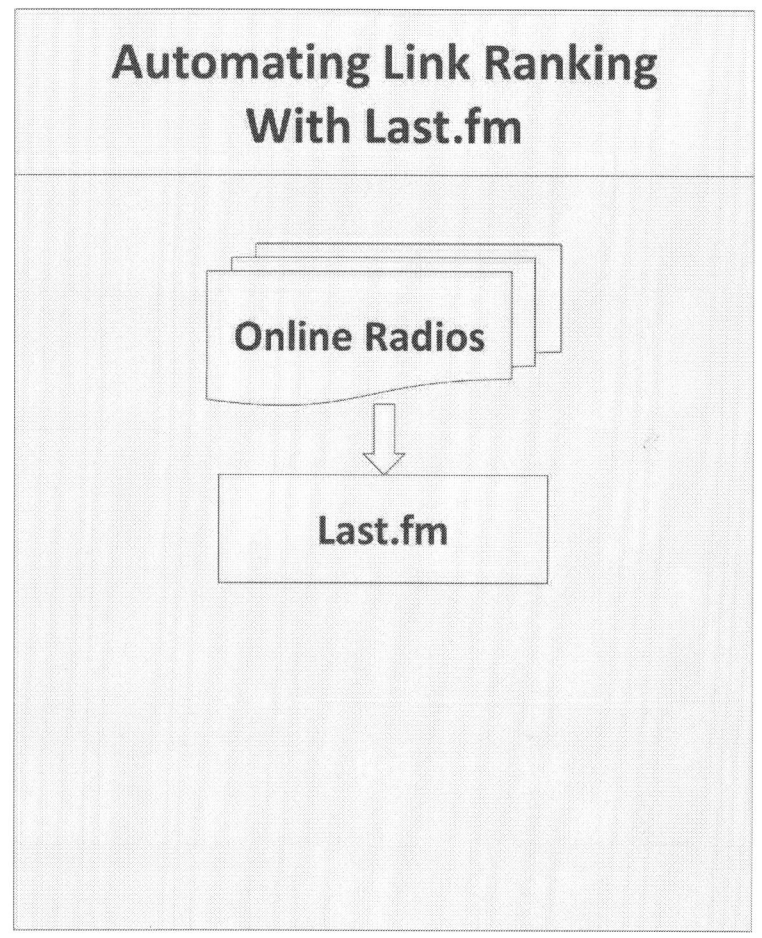

Figure 7: Last.fm Example Artist

Selena Gomez

Overview   Tracks   Albums   Photos

SCROBBLES   LISTENERS

28.6M   **810.3K**

    Escucha Selena Gomez

   POPULAR THIS WEEK
Fetish (feat. Gucci Man
13,608 listeners

   LATEST RELEASE
Fetish
1 track

There are two ways to work with Last.fm is: the easy way and the hard way.

The easy way to work with last.fm:

First, get an email address. Then, get accounts in Spotify and Last.fm. Finally, being logged in Spotify and Last.fm, go to Spotify settings and connect your account with that of Last.fm. As a result, each time you play a song in Spotify, the data of that song will appear automatically on Last.fm. This tactic will complement the one I explained before to rank online radios.

You can apply the same tactic with Deezer, but with a small difference, you need another email to register in Deezer and Last.fm because if you play music from two or more radios and "scroble" to Last.fm, the latter will show statistics only from one of the radios not from all ones.

The main advantage of Last.fm is that it allows documenting your music once this one starts to appear. In fact, you can add the artist's biography, single's or album's description as well as photos or artwork. Don't forget to add keywords as music type and genre. For example, you may describe "Your love song" as a "piece of love music composed in the ballad genre."

Another benefit is that Last.fm is a social network, so you can follow fans with the same musical taste than you.

The Massive Way to Work with Last.fm

As I mentioned before, we have to promote our music in many radios. Therefore, to promote all of them simultaneously, we have to follow the next steps:

First, get as many email address as radios you want to promote. Then, get accounts in as many radios you want to work at the same time. With each email, get an account with Last.fm. After that, connect each radio with Last.fm. Finally, in a browser open as many tabs as radios you have accounts, log into them, and start to listen to your music. All of them will share your music statistics in Last.fm automatically, giving your music more popularity.

Last.fm supports the following radios (2)

- 8tracks
- Amazon Music
- Deezer
- Google Play Music
- Groove music
- Hype Machine
- iTunes
- Pandora
- Rhapsody
- Shazam
- Spotify
- Spotify Connect - (PS4, Sonos, Amazon Echo, Google Chromecast, and More...) via
- Tidal
- SoundCloud
- YouTube

Check the citation (2) to find out how to configure each radio with last.fm.

Automate Link Building with This Free Powerful Tool that Nobody is Telling You

IFTTT (https://ifttt.com) stands for "if this, then that." This is a free online service that allows connecting events performed on websites or apps that propagate actions to other websites or apps. For example, if you play a song in Deezer, you can publish the song title, artist name, cover art image, and web address to a blog automatically.

Imagine the enormous power that you can achieve with this tool. You can connect everything with everything.

At the time of writing this book, there are the principal services:

Music

- Spotify
- Deezer
- SoundCloud

Blogging

- Blogger
- Tumblr
- Weebly
- WordPress

Bookmarking

- Bitly
- Delicious
- Diigo

- Pocket
- Buffer

Cloud storage

- Amazon Cloud Drive
- Box
- Dropbox
- Google Drive
- OneDrive
- OneDrive for Business
- QNAP
- Seagate Personal Cloud
- Verizon Cloud

Email

- Email
- Email Digest
- Gmail
- Office 365 Mail

Notes

- Evernote
- Memobird
- Nimbus Note
- Note widget
- OneNote

Social networks

- Ello
- Facebook
- Facebook Pages
- Foursquare
- Instagram
- Instawell

- LinkedIn
- Pinterest
- Reddit
- Sina Weibo
- Twitch
- Twitter

To use this website you need only one email to register for IFTTT.com and the other web properties, but you can use the emails created in previous step as well. In this book I won't focus on teach you how to use IFTTT, instead, I will focus on strategy. Indeed, there are many good tutorials to learn how to use IFTTT. Here some links:

- https://www.slideshare.net/AnneUy3/tutorial-how-to-use-ifttt-and-ifttt-applets
- https://www.slideshare.net/JenroseArellano2/iftt t-basic-tutorial
- https://www.YouTube.com/watch?v=b0xBfk1WV 0g
- https://www.YouTube.com/watch?v=DJ2ZHAQhA qc

Before explain how to use IFTT to promote your music inventory, I will classify the websites described above in 2 categories

Sources of Information

Sources of Information are those website that contains your money site links. Among them, you can include:

- Spotify
- Deezer
- SoundCloud
- Blogger

- Tumblr
- Weebly
- WordPress

SEO amplifiers

SEO amplifiers are the rest websites. Those websites allow creating "SEO noise" or backlinks to your main websites or money websites, improving your ranking in search results.

The objective is to create backlinks from different websites pointing to your money sites. You can see the architecture in Figure 8:

Figure 8: Architecture of – Link Ranking

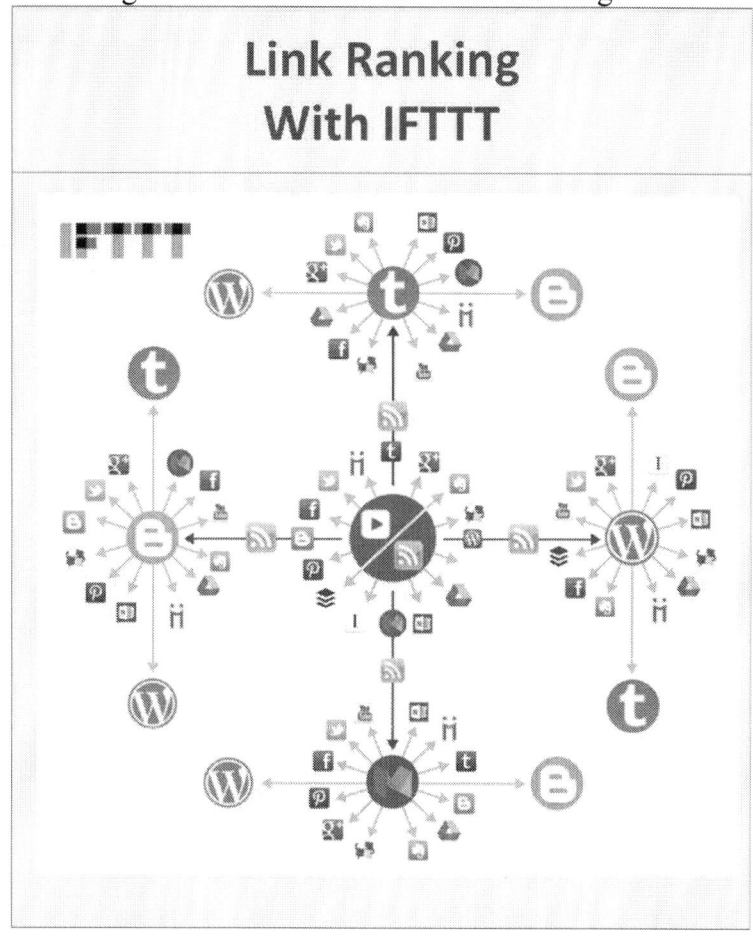

Automatic Link Building with Deezer

IFTTT allows you to capture user events on Deezer and perform actions in other websites such as social networks. The Deezer input events are the following;

- New favorite track: This trigger fires every time you add a track to your favorites.
- New favorite album: This trigger fires every time you add an album to your favorites.
- New favorite artist: This trigger fires every time you add an artist to your favorites.
- New favorite mix: This trigger fires every time you add a mix to your favorites.
- New played track: This trigger fires every time you have played a new track.
- New track added to playlist: This trigger fires every time you add a track in a selected playlist.

This tactic works as follows; You have to create an applet that connects an event from Deezer (such a new favorite of a track or album or artist) to a social bookmarking service or social network.

Let's say you create an applet that connects this Deezer event: "New favorite track," with the Diigo event: "post a link." After that, if you favorite a track in rhat radio, then IFTTT automatically will post the link of that song in the bookmarking site.

In addition, you have to create multiple applets to connect each one of the Deezer events with the bookmarking sites Bitly, Pocket, and Buffer, respectively. Moreover, you can create other applets where with the same Deezer events connecting with social networks such as Facebook, Twitter, Instagram, etc. View Figure 9.

Figure 9: Example of an IFTTT connection

Remember, you have to create each receipt one by one but once. For example:

- If new favorite track place a link in Diigo.
- If new favorite album place a link in Diigo.
- If new favorite Artist place a link in Diigo.
- If new favorite track place a link in Bitly.

- If new favorite album place a link in Bitly.
- If new favorite Artist place a link in Bitly.
- If new favorite track place a link in Pocket.
- If new favorite album place a link in Pocket.
- If new favorite Artist place a link in Pocket.
- Etc.

In general:

- If new event in Deezer place a link in a social bookmarking site.
- If new favorite album place a link in a social network.
- If new favorite Artist place a link in a document sharing service.

Be sure to configure IFTTT applets to show the title, link and photo of your artist, single or album for better engagement.

Don't be afraid for the apparent complexity of working with IFTTT. On the contrary, it is a very easy process. You set this up once, and it will last forever. The setup of the whole process can last just a couple of hours. Then, but this tool will do the job for you. Indeed, this tool will work with your current releases as well as your future ones. However, if you don't have time, and you can afford the price you can outsource this process to freelancers. I will show you where to hire freelancers in the resource's section of this book.

Automatic Link Building with Spotify

Unfortunately, at the time of writing this book, IFTTT launched a new version eliminated many Spotify events that previously existed, they were similar to those of Deezer. Just let's wait Spotify adds more events to its IFTTT receipts.

Currently, IFTTT supports two Spotify events:

- New saved track: This Trigger fires every time you save a new track to Your Music on Spotify.
- New track added to a playlist: This Trigger fires every time a new track is added to a playlist you specify.

Even though this scarcity, these two events are powerful enough to create backlinks to your music pages in the similar way I explained for Deezer, and in this way to increase its rank in search engines.

The applets are similar to those of Deezer. Just add the Spotify events. You need to connect your services to IFTTT and start to save your tracks.

Automatic Link Building with the Rest of Online Radios and Stores

Unfortunately, there are no direct connection between the rest of radios and stores and IFTTT. However, you can use indirectly in this way: Just create a blog post in free services such as Blogger, WordPress, or Tumbler and connect them with the rest of services (Figure 10). Do this before write anything. Finally, write a post with the title of your single or album, the link, and the artwork. I recommend you to add the genre and topic of the song. It is not need to be a great blog post, just be descriptive, because this post is not for humans but for search engines. For example:

- If new blog post you write about your Apple Music in **Blogger** post a link in a bookmark website such as Diigo, Bitly, Pocket or Buffer
- If new blog post you write about your Apple Music in **WordPress** post a link in a bookmark website such as Diigo, Bitly, Pocket or Buffer
- If new blog post you write about your Apple Music in **Tumblr** post a link in a bookmark website such as Diigo, Bitly, Pocket or Buffer
- In general, if new blog post you write about your music from any radio or store (Apple Music/Amazon/Google Play, etc.) in Blogger/WordPress/Tumblr post a link in a bookmark website such as Diigo, Bitly, Pocket or Buffer.
- The same for social networks, if a new blog post you write about your music from any radio or store (Apple Music/Amazon/Google Play, etc.) in Blogger/WordPress/Tumblr post a link in a bookmark website such as Facebook, Twitter, Instagram or Pinterest.

You can share the content of these blogs in two ways:

- Directly via IFTTT receipts.
- Via feeds to this other sharing service DLVR.IT.

Figure 10: Link building with blogs and ITTT/DLVR

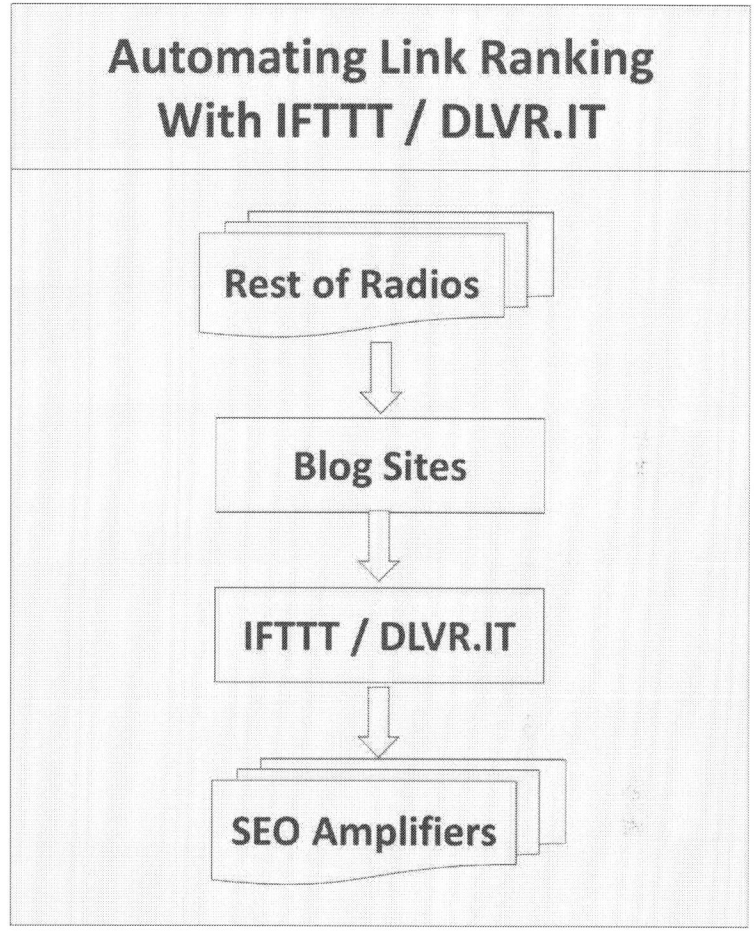

In the second case, here I show you how get the feeds from the following blog services:

In Blogger, let's say your blog is named "my-rock-songs.blogspot.com" the feed address will be:

- http:// my-rock-songs.blogspot.com/feeds/posts/default

In WordPress, let's say your blog is named "my-rock-songs.wordpress.com" the feed address will be:

- my-rock-songs.wordpress.com/?feed=rss
- my-rock-songs.wordpress.com/?feed=rss2
- my-rock-songs.wordpress.com/?feed=rdf
- my-rock-songs.wordpress.com/?feed=atom

In Tumblr, let's say your blog is named "my-rock-songs.tumblr.com" the feed address will be:

- https:// my-rock-songs.tumblr.com/rss

Don't be intimidated for the apparent complexity of this tactic. IFTTT is a very powerful tool and is free. As homework, signup in IFTTT and make some connections to practice.

To write posts in social networks such as Facebook or Google plus you will need this "feeds to post" tool: dlvr.it. This tool is fermium so you can use it to post up to 10 links per day.

Here is a tutorial how to use Dlvr.it:

https://www.YouTube.com/watch?v=bxmP3XTPseM

You can find more tutorials in YouTube.

Automatic Link Building From Cloud Storage and Online Notes

Online drives are sites such as Box, Dropbox, Google Drive and similar. The formula is to create one directory, share it publicly, get the link, and index it in the services from Part II. Finally, create the following applet in IFTTT:

- if a new favorite track, create a document in Google Drive (for example). Be sure you include the title, link, and photo of your music.

For Online Notes such as Evernote, Memobird, Nimbus Note, etc., the procedure is the same: create a folder; share it publicly, index the folder link. Then, for each event you want to capture, create a note in that folder.

How Get Links from SoundCloud and Similar Sites

As I stated before, you before you share your singles or tracks in sites as SoundCloud, you should register them first with any music distribution service, protecting in this way your copyright and royalties. Once done that, you can share your work in as many music sharing websites you can find. Most of these sites offer backlinks to your money sites so take advantage of that feature.

Getting Backlinks from YouTube

YouTube is a great place to promote your music. However, as I explained before regarding the music sharing sites, be sure you get your YouTube Content id before publishing your music videos there. When you submit your music, you should take advantage of the description section of the video service to give a summary of your music and post all your music money links there.

Getting Backlinks from This News Social Network

Reddit (https://www.reddit.com) is a very popular website that consists of communities around topics. It has a big and enthusiastic music community where you can participate sharing your music links. Here you have a couple of Reddit tutorials:

- https://www.YouTube.com/watch?v=ENUpkTVY6gA
- https://www.YouTube.com/watch?v=toc2S1-BMlo

Be sure to post your music links in a music related community like this:

- https://www.reddit.com/r/Music/

Before posting your links read the guidelines of the community and respect the rules.

Share Your Music in The Social Network that Google Loves

This is Google Plus (https://plus.google.com). Yes, it is not as popular as Facebook, but it is a Google property, and it will give your links more rank in its search engine. There are two ways to post automatically in Google Plus wall:

- In IFTT. indirectly, via Buffer.com. Create an account in Buffer, connect your Google Plus account, and then in IFTTT, connect Deezer or Spotify events with Google Plus via Buffer.

- In DLVR.IT you can connect blogs such as Blogger, WordPress, Tumblr or any that supports feeds directly with Google Plus wall.

Currently, there is no way to post automatically to Google Plus groups, you have to do manually or hire any freelancer described in the resources section,

Share Your Music in This New Social Network

No, it is not Facebook. It is Minds.com. I do not have doubts about the popularity of Facebook. However, in the last years, this old social network has become a sort of mercenary website. It charges you money to share your content with your fans.

On the contrary, Minds.com remunerates you with points each time you use this social network and participate in discussions. Then, you can use the accumulated points to advertise your content. In addition, this social network has a strong and growing music community where you can share your work. I think you should give a try.

Currently, it is impossible to automate posts in Minds. You have to do manually.

Another New Social Network Exclusively for Musicians

Join the bartering economy, just when I was finishing this book, I received an invitation from this new social network: **Drooble** (https://drooble.com). Drooble aims exclusively to musicians and fans. Similarly to

Minds.com, this website remunerates you with points each time you participate sharing posts, comments or music.

In addition you can interchange services without money. For example, you can get mastering services for your music and you give in exchange your music skills to another artist or band.

You also can earn money reviewing other artists songs.

Finally, after gathering enough points, you can exchange those with advertising.

Tips to Share Your Music in Facebook

To post your links, you should choose groups over wall and pages for engagement. Indeed, you can have thousands of music groups to share your links. It'd better if you create your own groups. Facebook allows automating posts in your groups but doesn't in other groups. In alien groups, you should post your links manually, if you automate them in other groups, your account can be banned.

To create your groups use the following policy: use engaging names to attract people. For example, apply names such as: "Promote your romantic songs in this group" or "Promote your folk music here" or both. Remember groups are free. Test as many names as you believe and after some time, delete the losers.

To automate post in your groups, you should use Dlvr.it instead of IFTTT. IFTTT only allows posting links on your wall and pages but not on groups.

Dlvr.it allows to post in all of them. Register yourself in Dlvr.it. Then, connect your Facebook account. Finally, connect your Blogger, WordPress or Tumblr feeds with the created social network profile. Remember that the free level of Dlvr.it only let 10 daily posts

The Secret Music Marketing Technique to Get Listeners in Radios

Throughout this book, I explained you how promote your music links to get better visibility in search engines. These techniques are necessary. However, there is a better way to get permanent listeners. This is through the use of **playlists**. Indeed, music fans use to listen to one song once. On the other hand, playlists are forever. There are more chances that a fan subscribes to a playlist than listen to one song and save it. In addition, listening to a playlist creates many streams of income than listening to only a song.

Creating playlists is an art. However, they are free in all radios so you can experiment with them. Here is my experience: Create playlist with the name of the genre or the topic of your music. For example, create playlist with the name: "My best love songs" or "Best folk songs playlist", assuming you composed a love song in the folk genre. Then, add around one-third or one-half of the best songs of the same topic or genre from the radio rankings. Next, add your own songs to the playlist. Finally, apply the same techniques described previously in this book; link collection, link Indexing, and link ranking, to promote it in search engines. Hopefully, you will attract the fans of the other songs to yours.

Here is an example:

- Best music for concentration and studying: http://open.spotify.com/user/goodvibras/playlist/6sgWlrEGODOgBZH1e4koEb

Remember that creating playlists is a manual process, but the promotion can be automated. They are available in all radios and are free. Just try to experimenting creating and promoting one at the time. Indeed, you have to promote playlists as you did with your music links.

What to Expect and Some Results

In the Figure 11, I show the plays from Spotify. I have around 120 songs among singles and tracks form four groups. The results are irregular because I tried many tactics to promote my music. I apply SEO since 2014, SEO is about traffic, and the figure shows plays. Therefore, traffic does not mean necessary plays, there is a conversion rate. This means that from 100 visitors your music links receive, they may get around 20 or 30 plays. Even though it is difficult to predict how many plays you may get for your music, once you start the SEO work, there is a notorious improvement in the number of streams. Moreover, I do neither concerts nor presentations, just pure SEO and Social Media Marketing. Another advantage for SEO is that you work only one for some period. It can take some weeks or months on autopilot, but the effects are permanent. Indeed, you will get a perpetual cash flow.

Figure 11: Spotify Plays

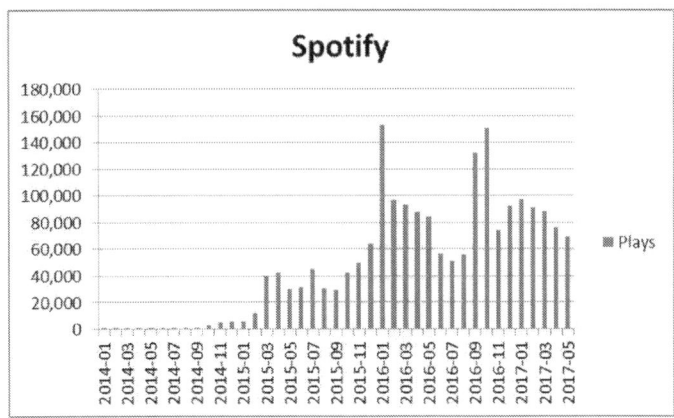

In Figure 12, I show the plays in Apple Music, here the results are less impressive because this radio has not the free level than Spotify has, but the SEO and Social Media effect are notorious over time. I must say that Social Media Marketing is a matter of another book.

Figure 12: iTunes Plays

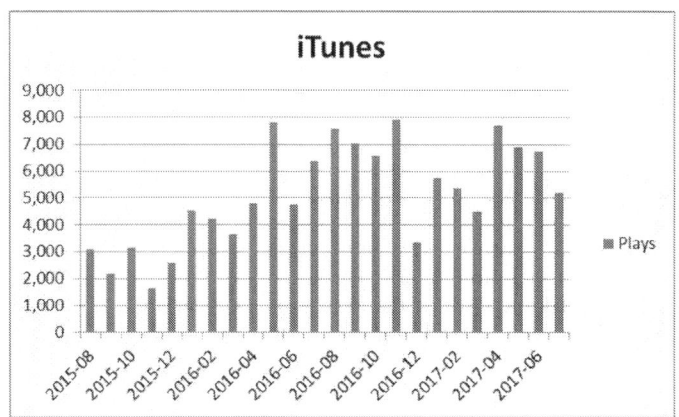

In Figure 13, I show the plays for Deezer, it appears in concordance with the market share showed in Figure 3.

Figure 13: Deezer Plays

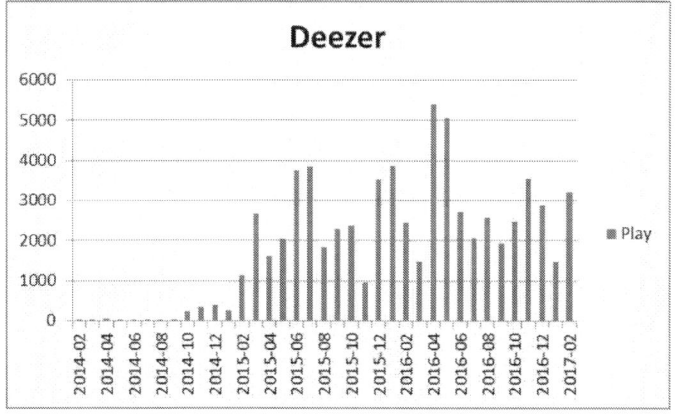

In conclusion, SEO may improve your steams in the long-term. However, it is a slow process and it takes some time to observe the effects. I must add that SEO is not exclusive; it may be part of a marketing mix along with paid advertisement, press releases, concerts and presentations. I reiterate, if you are new in the music business SEO is a good way to start to promote your music.

YouTube The jewel or the Crown

The last two graphics (Figures 14 and 15) refer to traffic and income from YouTube. This property is the most important source for musicians. Even the low pay per stream rate, the big amount of users compensates this shortcoming. As I stated before, you should get the Content Id for your music. Paradoxically, you do not need to anything with YouTube, because it is a search engine itself. However, creating your own videos and if getting traffic to them, will help to increase your royalties.

Figure 14: YouTube Plays

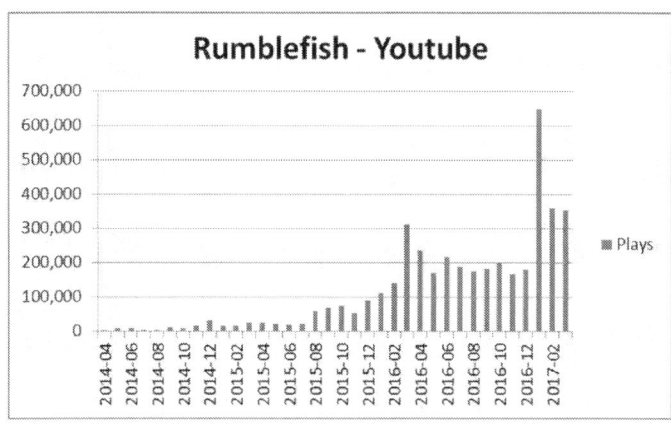

Figure 15: YouTube Royalties (Via Rumblefish)

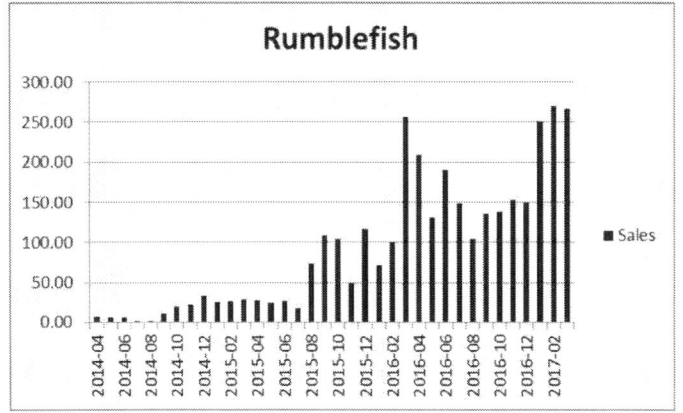

Getting Additional Links

As last recommendation, I suggest you take advantage of any source for backlinks that you can find, especially those from Google properties. Get backlinks from your own Google Profile, Pages, and Groups. This work is manual but rewarding in the long-term. Watch these videos to get inspired (no need to buy anything);

https://youtu.be/LYpnm5nQlLo

https://youtu.be/kuSj8eLumpw

https://youtu.be/9nJxAxp3-xw

Summary for Part 3: Link Ranking

After reading this third part of the book, you can start to rank your music properties. Link ranking is a never-ending process. Therefore, do not desperate, be patience and start working on a web property at the time. Start with a radio first, then, work with a single. After that, with more experience, start to work with an album and so on. You can dedicate 15 minutes a day per-link in your own benefit.

In a near future, if you wish, when you start receiving more royalties from your music, you can invest a part of the money in outsourcing the process to freelancers for those web properties still not profitable. Just remember: each link with your music is a potential source of income.

No matter the path you take, if you start to work in SEO for your music web properties, the outcome will always be an endless cash flow.

Resources for Part 3: Link Ranking

(1) Last.fm. Retrieved May 17, 2017, from
https://en.wikipedia.org/wiki/Last.fm
(2) Last.fm. Retrieved May 07, 2017, from
https://www.last.fm/about/trackmymusic

Part 4: Bonuses and Resources

Bonuses for Owners of Websites

Throughout the book, I didn't touch the topic of SEO for website owners. I didn't do that for one main reason: I don't recommend starting one. Indeed, owning a website today is too complex for one person, especially if you are a beginner. It requires technical skills such as: securing the server to avoid hacking, to configure SSL (Secured Socket Layer) to protect users, to work with AMP (Accelerated Mobile Pages) to make your website faster, to make it desktop and mobile friendly, besides programming skills. Even worse, Google made mandatory the use of SSL and APM if you want to rank your website. Of course, you can outsource the website building, but it will be expensive. In addition, you never will be able to compete with big players such the online radio and stores mentioned in this book.

However, there are many musicians that have successful websites and make enough sales to cover their costs. If you have a website or plan to have one, contact me to send you **free** two additional eBooks about how optimize your own websites to this mail;

mhonores@iuj.ac.jp

Or contact via the Facebook group.

Resources

Group for support and questions about this Book

Facebook group: SEO for Musicians

https://www.facebook.com/groups/seoformusicians/

Free tools for web scraping

Web scrapers are extensions for the Chrome browser that allows you to collect your web properties easily. Go to Chrome Store (https://chrome.google.com) and search for "web scraper" or "web scraping" extensions Install, watch the videos, and start to scrap your music links.

Freelancer services to get links

- Spotify links

https://www.fiverr.com/mentallion/give-you-your-sporify-links-for-seo

- iTunes links:

https://www.fiverr.com/mentallion/give-you-your-itunes-links

- Deezer links

https://www.fiverr.com/mentallion/give-you-your-deezer-links

- For Amazon links contact the author

For a complete SEO for Musicians Package click here:

https://www.fiverr.com/mentallion/give-you-a-seo-for-musicians-package

- Resources to build IFTTT networks:

Just go to Fiverr.com and search the term: "IFTTT."

- For more music promotion services:

Go to Fiverr.com go to the section: Digital Marketing / Music Promotion. I recommend gigs to post to Facebook/Google Plus groups and link building in high authority sites.

Warnings

In Fiverr, you should buy only the most popular services. Avoid black hat ones such as bot playing, massive link building, or increase artificially your ranks in Google. Before hiring services, you can ask in the Facebook group for my two cents advice,

32311100R00054

Printed in Poland ·
by Amazon Fulfillment
Poland Sp. z o.o., Wrocław